"ZOYA"

"A GIRL'S POETIC JOURNEY"

NAVEEN DUBEY

Made with ❤ on the Notion Press Platform
www.notionpress.com

To all the little girls of India,

You are strong, you are brave, and you are capable of anything. You are the future of this great nation. You have the power to drive change and create a better future for all of us.

This book is dedicated to all of you and may you always be fearless and unstoppable.

With love and admiration,

Naveen Dubey

Contents

Foreword *vii*

Preface *ix*

Acknowledgements *xi*

Prologue *xiii*

1. The Paradise 1
2. A Winter Wonderland 2
3. A Little Girl 3
4. Shining Bright: The Joyful Life Of A Little Girl 4
5. Winter Wonders With Zoya 5
6. A Tale Of Friendship 6
7. Zoya's Lamb 7
8. A Heart Filled With Song 8
9. Reunion: A Blessing From The Goddess 9
10. Waiting For Daddy 11
11. The Mother 12
12. A Little Girl's Dream 13
13. Heroic Return 14
14. Until We Meet Again 15
15. A Tale Of Courage In A Stormy Night 16
16. A Summer Day Of Joy 17
17. Shikara 18
18. A Brave New Start 19
19. The Sweet Summer Treats 20
20. Goodbye, Grandma 21
21. "from Valley's Warmth To Delhi's Cold: Zoya's Journey Of Loss And Hope" 22

Contents

22. A Story Of Home And Heart 23

23. The Change 24

24. Beauty's Curse 25

25. "zoya: A Tale Of Love And Beauty" 26

26. Zoya's Kashmiri Memories: Love, Loss, And Remembrance 27

27. Zoya: A Beacon Of Hope And Resilience In Pursuit Of Her Dream 28

28. Picking Up The Pieces 29

29. A Tale Of Friendship And Resilience 30

30. Zoya's Circle Of Life 31

Be Brave And Strong 33

Foreword

Discover the touching journey of Zoya, from the delights of childhood to the challenges of adulthood, in this poignant collection of poetry. Explore the intricate themes of family, friendship, and love, and relive the experiences of a young girl. Be inspired by Zoya's self-discovery and her unwavering determination, and be moved by her poignant story. Find the courage to take control of your own destiny, and gain a fresh appreciation of life and its possibilities through this remarkable work. Congratulations to the author for their exquisite portrayal of Zoya's story, and happy reading to all.

- Chat GPT

Preface

To

The Readers,

During my visit to Kashmir in 2005, I had the good fortune of meeting Zoya, an incredible young girl. Her spirit, kindness, and determination captured my heart. This book is my tribute to Zoya, weaving together her life story from childhood in the valley to her remarkable journey in adulthood. It is a testament to her courage, resilience, and hope in the face of adversity.

Zoya's strength and resilience in the face of life's challenges are an inspiration to us all, and this book is a beautiful testament to the power of the human spirit. Through this work, I aim to capture the essence of Zoya and the beauty of Kashmir and its people. I hope you enjoy reading it as much as I enjoyed writing it.

Naveen Dubey

Acknowledgements

I would like to express my deepest gratitude to the creators of **Chat GPT (OpenAI-API)** for enabling me to create a masterpiece that has a unique fusion of technology and creativity. Without your help, this would not have been possible. Your innovative and creative approach to technology has made a significant impact in the world of literature. Your contributions have been invaluable, and I thank you for your tremendous efforts.

I am also grateful to all the people who supported me along the way, including my parents Shri S.P Dubey and Mrs. Pushpa Dubey, and my wife **Surabhi**. I would also like to thank my editors, publishers, my friends and everyone who believed in me and my vision.

Last, but not least, I would like to thank all the readers who will take the time to read this book. Your support is the greatest reward for my hard work. Thank you all for making this book possible.

Naveen Dubey

Prologue

Dear reader,

Through this book, the author aims to showcase how AI can be used creatively to complement human creativity and enhance the storytelling experience. The use of AI to generate titles and verses may be a novel concept, but it is just one example of how technology can be used to push the boundaries of traditional storytelling. The author hopes that this experiment will inspire others to explore the possibilities of AI in creative fields and to approach storytelling in innovative ways. Ultimately, this book is a testament to the beauty and power of human imagination and the potential of technology to augment it.

This book is a unique experiment that uses Artificial Intelligence (AI) to generate titles and some verses, including the first poem entirely created by AI (Chat-GPT). The story is about a young girl from the Valley of Kashmir, whom I met at the age of 5. I was struck by her innocence and zest for life and wanted to preserve those memories. I hope that readers will enjoy the girl's journey as much as I enjoyed documenting it. In conclusion, I believe that this book is a groundbreaking and creative project that readers will appreciate.

1. The Paradise

A paradise so divine,
A beauty so sublime,
That's the Kashmir valley for you,
A sight so beautiful, so true.
A heaven on earth,
A blessing from birth,
A place so serene,
Where you can find peace and mirth.
The snow covered mountains,
The lush green meadows,
The blue sky above,
A place you'll always love.
The Dal and Nagin lakes,
The serene calmness of the place,
The graceful willow trees,
A sight so heavenly and grace.
The saffron fields,
The sparkling rivers,
The fragrant flowers,
A sight that will always linger.
The snow capped peaks,
The majestic landscapes,
The beauty of Kashmir,
It's a blessing that's never to miss.

2. A Winter Wonderland

Winter has come,
The snow is falling,
The sky is grey,
The branches swaying.
The cold winds blow,
The trees are bare,
No birds song,
The air is still and rare.
The snowflakes twinkle,
The night is clear,
The fire is warm,
And the stars so near.
The snowman's smile,
The joy of children,
The cold winter days,
Oh, what a wonderful season!

3. A Little Girl

Softly, the sun warms the Kashmir Valley,
Illuminating the beauty of a little girl.
Her skin as delicate as a petal,
And her eyes, pure as a pearl.
Her hair, like a cascade of night,
Flows gracefully down her back.
A sight that takes one's breath away,
One that one cannot lack.
The beauty of this gentle soul,
Is one that can't be denied.
Her spirit so pure and so whole,
She is truly a delight.
She moves with grace and poise,
Her laughter, so sweet and pure.
Her innocence is a joy that no one can destroy,
Her beauty, beyond compare.
The enchanting beauty of Kashmir,
Is seen in this little girl.
Her beauty is a blessing,
One that will forever swirl.

4. Shining Bright: The Joyful Life of a Little Girl

A little girl with a gleaming smile
She lights up the room from miles
She's curious and funny and wise
She'll bring joy wherever she flies
Her laughter so sweet,
her eyes so bright
She brings joy and peace to the night
She is filled with love and so much care
A little girl with so much to share
Her innocence and beauty so true
It's a wonder she can so easily do
The things she does to make us all smile
She's a little girl with such a style
A little girl with so much to give
She'll show us a life that we can live
A life of joy and of fun
A little girl, our special one

5. Winter Wonders with Zoya

Zoya, a little girl, with a smile so sweet
Enjoys her days in winter's heat
The chilly winter winds of Kashmir blow
But Zoya's happiness never slows
She loves to play in the snow
In her heart a winter glow
She skips and sings, she looks around
At the beauty winter has found
In the market she goes to buy
Her favorite winter treats so high
The snowman she builds, with her little hands
A sight so beautiful, one understands
The winters of Kashmir, so cold and white
But Zoya's heart so warm and bright
She loves the winter, the snow, the trees
The cold winter air, she loves to breathe
And so she plays, she laughs, she smiles
In the winters of Kashmir, her love beguiles.

6. A Tale of Friendship

Once was a little girl named Zoya
She was young, and so full of joy
Her life was so full of happiness
So much love to share and enjoy
One of her favorite things to do
Was to take her little lamb for a stroll
Through the meadow and around the town
Wherever she wanted to go
The lamb was special to her, Her only friend in life
She loved to take it everywhere
And keep it close by her side
The lamb was her constant companion
It went everywhere with her
Through the fields and over the hills
It was always there to cheer
The little girl Zoya,
and her little lamb
Were the closest of friends
And they'd always be there for each other
No matter what life would bring

7. Zoya's Lamb

Oh sweet Zoya, what a sad sight,
For her lamb had been taken in the night.
In the morning she awoke to find,
That her dear lamb had been taken away from behind.
What was once a bond so strong,
Had been taken away, and it felt so wrong.
The little girl was so sad and blue,
For her lamb had been taken away from her too.
She said a prayer for her dear friend,
In the hope that he would be found in the end.
She held his memories close to her heart,
And prayed for the day that they wouldn't be apart.
The little girl was full of hope,
That she'd find her lamb and not have to mope.
But until that day, she held on tight,
To the memories of her precious lamb in the night.

8. A Heart Filled with Song

Little girl Zoya sitting sad on the bank of the lake
Her eyes filled with tears, her heart filled with ache.
As she looks around, no one can see,
The sadness that overwhelms her and sets her free.
The wind blows through her hair, and she shivers in its embrace.
The coolness of the lake comforts her, but its stillness brings her no peace.
Her thoughts are spinning, her fears too strong.
And she can't help but feel that something's wrong.
She sits there in the stillness, her heart feeling heavy.
Trying to make sense of the world, and be ready.
She feels so alone, her heart so broken.
She needs someone to talk to, a word to be spoken.
But alas, she is alone, and no one is near.
She looks up at the sky and whispers a prayer.
To find the courage to carry on, and to be strong.
Little girl Zoya, her heart filled with song.

9. Reunion: A Blessing from the Goddess

Zoya, a little girl so young and fair
Had lost her lamb, her sadness was so rare
Searching for her lost lamb near the lake
She saw a goddess arise from the deep
The goddess said, 'I know of your plight
Your lost lamb is safe, I will make it right
Take my hand, and I will lead Your lost lamb will follow you with speed'
Zoya took the goddess' hand with care
The goddess smiled and said, 'Do not despair
Your lamb will be returned to you soon
And your sadness will be gone, I can assure you'
The goddess brought the lamb back to Zoya's side
And Zoya's tears of sadness quickly dried
The little girl hugged the lamb tight
And thanked the goddess with all her might
The goddess smiled and said, 'Take care
Your lamb will always be there
It is a part of your family
And will always be a part of your destiny'
And so the goddess returned to the lake
Leaving Zoya and her lamb in her wake
Grateful for the kindness of the goddess

Zoya and her lamb continued on their blessedness.

10. Waiting for Daddy

Little girl Zoya, sitting at her door
Waiting for her father to come home once more
He's fighting in a far off war
And she's waiting so patiently
Her little heart is filled with fear
Will her father ever reappear?
Her days are long, her nights are short
But she never gives up hope
As the weeks and months go by
Zoya never lets out a sigh
She looks up at the night sky
And prays for her daddy
The days are getting longer and the nights are getting shorter
But Zoya's courage and hope still make her stronger
Her faith never fades, her hope will never die
As she waits for her father to come home and say hi

11. The Mother

Little girl Zoya looked around,
At the childrens loved by their mother,
She felt so lost and all alone,
For her mother had died, no other.
She wanted her mother by her side,
To take her hand and show her the way,
To tell her stories and kiss her goodnight,
To be with her all through out the day.
But Zoya stood there filled with grief,
For her mother was no more,
She wished she could hug her one last time,
But that was something she could not ignore.
Though Zoya stands alone in her sorrow,
She keeps her mothers memory in her heart,
For she knows deep inside that her mother will be watching her,
Though she's no longer here on this earth.

12. A Little Girl's Dream

Little girl zoya in the valley of Kashmir,
Dreams of the warmth of her mother and dad
Shivering in her cold bed all alone
Wishing for the days to soon come home
The snow falling gently on the hill
The wind blowing through her windowsill
The warmth of her family she does miss
The sound of the laughter she can only reminisce
The valley of Kashmir so far away
The little girl zoya in silent pray
Praying that one day she'll reunite
And feel the warmth of her family's light
She'll lay in her bed and close her eyes
Dream of the day when she won't have to cry
The little girl Zoya will be just fine
She'll be with her family in the valley of Kashmir in no time.

13. Heroic Return

He was a hero, brave and true
He'd gone to fight in the war so long
With his gun he'd done what he could do
To protect his country and his home
He'd been gone so very long
He'd been away from his daughter Zoya
She'd missed him so, her heart was gone
Not knowing if he'd ever come home
But one day, there was a knock at the door
The sound that little Zoya had longed to hear
Her father had returned, she'd never been more sure
She looked at him with a smile so sincere
The tears started to flow, her heart filled with joy
Father and daughter embraced, no more feeling alone
The war had taken so much, the pain of it all
But the love of a father had made Zoya whole
He was a hero, brave and true
He'd gone to fight in the war so long
His love had kept Zoya safe and sound
And their hearts were now forever bound

14. Until We Meet Again

Little Zoya, sweet and small,
Her father missing her mum of all,
Her mother died when she was three,
Hearts so broken, her family tree.
A father's love so strong and true,
A daughter's heart so fragile too,
He fills the void of her missing mum,
He's always there when the going's tough.
Yet still she longs to feel her hug,
To hear her mother's lullaby,
For that sweet embrace that can't be replaced,
Her heart still aches, but he'll try and take the place.
Though the days may seem long and hard,
Her dad will keep her safe and sound,
He'll never stop loving her unconditionally,
Until his daughter is safe and sound.

15. A Tale of Courage in a Stormy Night

On a stormy night, with the wind so strong,
They heard a little girl, singing her song.
Her Father and her pet lamb were by her side,
In the cold and the dark, they did abide.
The thunder roared and the lightning flashed,
The Father knew this would be a test.
His daughter, Zoya, was small and frail,
But her courage was immense and never did fail.
He held her close and promised to keep,
Her safe from harm, as he quietly wept.
He knew the storm was nothing to fear,
With her love and courage, they'd always be near.
He held her tight until the storm had passed,
No more thunder and lightning, just a summer breeze at last.
The Father and Zoya, with their pet lamb,
The little girl and her Father, safe and sound, the best they can.

16. A Summer Day of Joy

The little girl Zoya,
In a tulip flowers garden,
Playing with her lamb,
On a warm summer day,
The tulips in bloom,
The sun was shining bright,
The grass was so green,
A beautiful sight.
Zoya laughed and giggled,
As she played with her lamb,
And the tulips swayed in the breeze,
In the garden so grand.
Zoya was so happy,
Her laughter filled the air,
Her joy was contagious,
It was a sight so rare.
The lamb and Zoya,
Playing in the garden so fair,
The sun was shining,
The tulips in bloom everywhere.
This memory will stay with me,
Of the sweet little girl and her lamb,
Playing in the tulip flowers garden,
On a warm summer day.

17. Shikara

Little girl Zoya, so blissful and merry,
On a shikara, with Papa, Grandma, and a lamb so very;
They sail through the waters of Dal Lake, so serene,
The beauty of nature, that can be seen!
As the shikara glides through the lake,
The little girl looks up to her Papa, "Oh, what a great take!"
Grandma too, so proud of her little one,
Tells stories of the old days, that were so fun!
The lamb, an integral part of the family,
Goes around looking for tiny flowers, so lovely!
The little girl laughs, and so does her Papa,
As the lamb plays, so joyous and happy!
As the sun sets, and the stars come out,
The little girl and the lamb, kiss goodnight, no doubt;
The shikara, sails back to the shore,
The memory of this day, will be remembered forever more.

18. A Brave New Start

Zoya on her first day of school
Is anxious and missing her lamb
So much she wanted to bring him,
But the rules wouldn't let her in
Her heart was full of fear and dread
To leave her lamb behind her bed
But as she walked in the school hall,
She knew she must face it all
Though she was so brave and bold,
Her heart was heavy and cold
She faced the class, with a smile
And determined to go the extra mile
She made some new friends that day,
She felt less alone at play
Though her lamb will always be missed,
She knows she'll never be dismissed

19. The Sweet Summer Treats

Zoya loves her grand mother's treats,
So sweet and so divine,
A warmth that fills her heart,
As she takes each bite of delight.
Each sweet is crafted with love,
The taste so unique and sublime,
A magical treat for her taste buds,
A treasure of a lifetime.
Her grand mother's hands make wonders,
The aroma of the sweets fill her nose
A special treat every summer,
A memory that she never wants to lose.
Her grand mother's treats are special,
A prized possession that she loves,
A moment of pure bliss and joy,
That will stay with her forever.

20. Goodbye, Grandma

Little Zoya grieves,
For her grandmother's death,
In her heart she believes,
She had taken her last breath.
A sorrowful goodbye,
She watches her Grandma go,
In her heart she cries,
For all that she'll never know.
The world has become so cold,
No warmth for little Zoya,
Her Grandma's love untold,
Now she'll never know.
Thoughts of her Grandma,
Memories of her smile,
Little Zoya's heart is in a jam,
Her heart has no guile.
No more hugs and kisses,
The love and care she did send,
Little Zoya will now miss,
Her Grandma's love that had no end.

21. "From Valley's Warmth to Delhi's Cold: Zoya's Journey of Loss and Hope"

The little girl Zoya, her heart so sore,
In the Valley of Kashmir she could take no more,
Her grandmother who nurtured and loved her so,
Had passed on leaving Zoya feeling so low.
Her father a soldier, his duty so clear,
To Delhi he must go, yet his heart was not here,
For Zoya he must be strong, she knew it so well,
Though she could not help cry, as they said their farewell.
The bus ride seemed longer, Delhi drawing near,
She thought of the Valley, the life she held dear,
The snow capped mountains, the lush green fields,
The love of her grandmother, that she now must yield.
Delhi was their destination, an unknown place and time,
The little girl Zoya, with sadness in her eyes,
Her heart so heavy, yet she will try,
To make this her home, just her and her dad and I.

22. A Story of Home and Heart

A little girl zoya so sad and so blue,
Came from Kashmir to Delhi all new.
To a place so strange and so cold,
She felt so lonely, like she's been sold.
Missed the valley so much in her heart,
And all the things she used to do, so smart.
But most of all, she missed her lamb, T
he one she loved, the one so fam.
The memories of the valley so strong,
Kept her going through the day so long.
But she was brave, and never gave up,
Kept on going, not once did she stop.
Though she was away from home so far,
Her lamb was with her, wherever she are.

23. The Change

Zoya once a child, now grown up too
No more playing games, no more just having fun
Realizing the importance of life and time
She's trying to make her future shine
Loneliness overwhelms her when the night falls
Memories of carefree days, she recalls
The joy of growing up and the sorrow of growing old
The time flies by and her heart feels cold
No one to tell her stories she remembers
No one to laugh and cry with her, like before
All she has is herself to depend
To carry on and not to bend
But Zoya is still strong, she'll make it through
She'll find her way, despite what is true
She'll make her own future and destiny
She'll work hard and fulfill her dreams.

24. Beauty's Curse

A curse it is to be so beautiful,
For unwanted attention you get the full.
Stalkers and catcallers, they call out my name,
My beauty just invites their shame.
I'm followed wherever I go,
It's a curse to be so beautiful, you know.
Comments on my looks and the way I dress,
It's a curse to be so beautiful, I confess.
I try to keep my head down and ignore,
But this beauty just keeps me from being ignored.
I'm scared to walk at night, My beauty is a curse, a fight.
I hear the comments and feel the stares,
My beauty is a curse and I'm aware.
It's a curse to be so beautiful and fair,
But I must remember that beauty isn't my despair.

25. "Zoya: A Tale of Love and Beauty"

Oh sweet Zoya so young and fair
A beauty more precious than any rare
Her heart so pure, her love so true
Her spirit so kind, her eyes so blue
She once knew a love so sweet
In a place so far, yet so discreet
A love that held no bounds
One that soared on wings so sound
His embrace was gentle, his kiss was warm
The love between them, forever to form
Though the days may be long and the nights hard
Zoya's love will never fall apart
Her heart so full of love and care
A special kind that only Zoya could share

26. Zoya's Kashmiri Memories: Love, Loss, and Remembrance

Zoya, young and beautiful,
Reminiscing about her past,
A childhood spent in Kashmir Valley,
The death of her beloved mother,
Grandmother, so loving and kind,
Gone to her final rest,
Her little lamb, so sweet and mild,
Lost to her in the west.
Thoughts of her first love, so dear,
Lingering in her memory,
The smell of saffron in the air,
The sight of snow-clad mountains, so fair.
A life, so full of joy and love,
But now, it's all a distant past,
The memories of these moments,
Will forever last.

27. Zoya: A Beacon of Hope and Resilience in Pursuit of Her Dream

Zoya, the young girl with a beautiful heart,
Pursued her goal to become a Doctor with her determined heart,
Fighting against all odds,
She took a step forward in her quest for success,
Though it was difficult, she never gave up,
Every obstacle she faced, she stayed tough,
She was the one who made it possible,
To achieve her dreams with resilience and zeal,
Her hard work was finally paid off,
She got the degree and now she was a Doctor,
She was now the one she always wanted to be,
A Doctor who could help and bring a smile to many,
Zoya, the young girl, was an inspiration,
A Doctor who could be a beacon of hope and motivation!

28. Picking Up the Pieces

Softly she wept, as her heart bled
The wounds of her loss still left unsaid
The love she once had, now had gone
The boy she loved, had moved on
Grief, like a wave, had overcome her
The valleys of tears, she could no longer defer
The pain of losing her mother, her grandmother too
Had come back, but this time, she knew what to do
The reality of life had hit her hard
She'd have to fill the void, in her own backyard
No more could she hide, or run away
She had to face her fears and make her own way
Though her heart was aching and her soul was sore
She'd have to find the strength to open the door
To a world she'd never known before And embrace a new life, one filled with more

29. A Tale of Friendship and Resilience

The little lamb was so sweet and meek,
It trembled with fear on its feet.
But the little girl held it close and tight,
With a gentle smile that gave it light.
Zoya the doctor was young and kind,
And she held out her hand to find.
The little girl with a lamb in her arms,
Had a story of sadness and harms.
She told Zoya of her plight,
Of a home that had been set alight.
The lamb was her only friend and source,
Of comfort and love in a distant course.
Zoya was moved by the tale of woe,
And she treated the girl with a gentle glow.
She shared her own story of strife,
Of a home that had been taken away from her life.
The doctor and the girl soon shared a bond,
One of understanding, one beyond.
They embraced each other's fate,
And vowed to never give up, no matter the weight.

30. Zoya's Circle of Life

The young doctor Zoya had a vision in her mind,
A circle of life, her mission she had to find.
To help the needy, to show them love and care,
To bring a smile on the faces of those in despair.
To work for orphan kids, a life-long journey she chose,
To provide them with a safe and warm home.
To give them the chance to strive and grow,
To build a future, so they can shine and glow.
To make sure their dreams can take flight,
To ensure that they have all the light.
To show them the way when the path is dark,
To be their light that will never go stark.
The young doctor Zoya had a mission in her mind,
A circle of life, to bring a better life she will find.

Be Brave And Strong

Dear strong and brave girls,

You are the future and have the power to change the world. You are capable of amazing things and have the power to make a difference. Don't ever forget that. In the face of adversity, fight hard like Zoya and never give up. Take on every challenge with courage and strength and use them to create the life you want. You are capable of incredible things, so don't be afraid to go after your dreams. Believe in yourself and never give up.

Sincerely,

Naveen Dubey

Printed by Libri Plureos GmbH in Hamburg, Germany